Pterosaur Trouble

To my clever wife, Cheryl, and to my two wonderful children. (The whole world became more beautiful and more important when you came into it.)

ACKNOWLEDGMENTS:

My profound thanks to Cheryl Hebert, Isaac Loxton, Jason Loxton, Andre Hebert, David Patton, William Bull and Pat Linse for photographic assistance, wise insights and many other forms of help as well.

Additional thanks to my colleagues Pat Linse and Michael Shermer at *Skeptic* magazine (www.skeptic.com) for their wisdom, support and ongoing encouragement.

Special thanks to Darren Naish for his expert paleontological advice and for giving so generously of his time and knowledge.

Science consultant: Darren Naish

Kids Can Press acknowledges the financial support of the Government of Ontario, through the Ontario Media Development Corporation's Ontario Book Initiative; the Ontario Arts Council; the Canada Council for the Arts; and the Government of Canada, through the CBF, for our publishing activity.

Published in Canada by
Kids Can Press Ltd.
25 Dockside Drive
Toronto, ON M5A 0B5

Published in the U.S. by
Kids Can Press Ltd.
2250 Military Road
Tonawanda, NY 14150

www.kidscanpress.com

Edited by Valerie Wyatt
Designed by Julia Naimska

This book is smyth sewn casebound.
Manufactured in Tseung Kwan O, NT Hong Kong, China, in 10/2012 by Paramount Printing Co. Ltd.

CM 13 0 9 8 7 6 5 4 3 2 1

Library and Archives Canada Cataloguing in Publication

Loxton, Daniel, 1975–
      Pterosaur trouble / written by Daniel Loxton ; illustrated by Daniel Loxton with Jim W.W. Smith.

(Tales of prehistoric life)

ISBN 978-1-55453-632-0

1. Pterosauria—Juvenile literature. 2. Dinosaurs—Juvenile literature.
I. Smith, Jim W. W. II. Title. III. Series: Tales of prehistoric life.

QE862.P7L69 2013   j567.918   C2012-904396-6

Kids Can Press is a **LORUS** Entertainment company

TALES OF PREHISTORIC LIFE

Pterosaur Trouble

Daniel Loxton

Illustrated by Daniel Loxton
with Jim W.W. Smith

Kids Can Press

Quetzalcoatlus soared through the air like a giant kite. His wide wings caught the warm wind.

Down below him was forest, coastline and sea. He had traveled far, following the coast. Soon he would turn away from the sea and cross this great, green land.

The huge pterosaur hovered for an instant ... then dipped his wing tip and flew on his way.

Once, millions of years before, pterosaurs ruled the skies. They alone soared high above the treetops.

But now these giant flying reptiles shared the air with many noisy neighbors — small flying dinosaurs. The pterosaur ignored these creatures as they flocked and flapped around him on feathered wings. And he ignored their huge dinosaur cousins who padded heavily across the sand below.

He flew on. He was *Quetzalcoatlus*, one of the largest fliers the world would ever know.

Quetzalcoatlus left the sea behind and soared over the lush forest. That night he roosted on a cliff. At dawn, as the sun came up, he searched for a place to feed.

Below he spied a winding river – just the place for a fishy breakfast.

He hurtled down through the curving river canyon.

The huge shadow of the pterosaur streaked along the riverbank and flickered over the trees.

He was too big to go unnoticed.

Glittery eyes opened in the shade of the forest. A pile of feathery, sleepy forms roused themselves. They raised their heads and followed the shadow passing overhead. They clicked and cooed. They sounded curious. They sounded hungry.

Quetzalcoatlus braked for a landing. His great, slow wing beats rippled the surface of the river. And then he settled — a giraffe-sized giant landing as gently as a dragonfly.

He stalked slowly and quietly over the rocks. He tilted his head this way and that. His beak blazed like fire in the morning light. A warm breeze stirred the fine, hairlike fibers that covered his body.

Quetzalcoatlus preferred open places where he could stalk small animals — anything that walked or slithered. But what hungry traveler would turn up his beak at a river full of fish?

Nearby, a herd of thirsty *Triceratops* waded in the water. Each was as big as a delivery truck and armed with a set of pointed horns. But *Triceratops* were plant eaters and no threat to *Quetzalcoatlus*. He ignored them, and they left him to his fishing.

But wait — what was this? A small, feathered dinosaur approached *Quetzalcoatlus*. Hmmmm. Was it small enough to eat?

It came closer and closer. *Quetzalcoatlus* began to stir uneasily. Some instinct warned him that the creature was not behaving as prey should. Small as it was, it moved like it was the one doing the hunting, not the other way around.

Suddenly, from every direction came the sounds of skittering claws and chittering calls. *Quetzalcoatlus* whirled around. The little dinosaurs were everywhere! The pack of *Saurornitholestes* crept closer on every side. Their fierce, piercing cheeps made the pterosaur shrink back in alarm.

And then the pack of small, fierce dinosaurs attacked.

The pterosaur was no easy prey. He was ten times taller than his attackers. His massive beak was deadly sharp.

He stabbed wildly with his beak. The pack scattered and dodged. He lashed out with his powerful forelimbs, sending the small dinosaurs flying. They squawked through the air and splashed into the water.

The noise of the fight echoed over the river. The pterosaur HOOONNNKED in anger and fear. The *Saurornitholestes* shrieked and cheeped as they attacked again and again.

In the background, the herd of *Triceratops* bellowed in alarm and shook their great horns in the air.

Quetzalcoatlus was a towering giant, but sometimes numbers and fierceness count more than size. The fast and ferocious dinosaurs swarmed over the huge pterosaur. They bit with sharp teeth. They slashed with their hook-shaped claws.

For every *Saurornitholestes* knocked aside, two more jumped onto the struggling giant. He twisted and whirled, stumbled and lurched, trying to shake them off. But there were too many to fight. He had to escape.

Crouching low on all four limbs, the pterosaur gathered his strength ... then he shoved forward with his powerful hind legs and upward with his long forelimbs. He was airborne!

Quetzalcoatlus launched into a lumbering, low flight, carrying two of his attackers with him. His vast wings unfolded and urgently beat the air. WHOOSH, WHOOSH, WHOOSH!

He flew toward the *Triceratops* herd. WHOOSH! WHOOSH! He struggled and strained to climb higher. One *Saurornitholestes* fell spinning into the water. But another clung tightly to the pterosaur's hairlike pelt.

The *Triceratops* bellowed. Their horns were like spikes. And *Quetzalcoatlus* was hurtling straight toward them.

Swiiiiiiiiisshhhhhh! The pterosaur skimmed over the *Triceratops*. The thin skin of his wings brushed over their sharp horns.

But what was that thump? *Quetzalcoatlus* soared to safety, leaving his unwelcome passenger stuck on the frill of the biggest, toughest, grouchiest *Triceratops* in the herd. The little *Saurornitholestes* squeaked in fear. The hulking, horn-headed dinosaurs closed in around him.

Quetzalcoatlus flew free and safe, high above the trees.
The cuts on his body hurt, but he would recover.

In front of him, the great, green forest stretched away
to the horizon. Up he flew and onward, out over that wild
land. He had a long way to go.

But first, there was the matter of breakfast.

Quetzalcoatlus and Saurornitholestes

Pterosaurs lived during the time of the dinosaurs. They were distantly related to the dinosaurs, but they were not dinosaurs. Nor were they birds. They were giant flying reptiles.

Quetzalcoatlus (Ket-sol-koe-AT-luss) was a huge type of pterosaur. In fact, it was quite possibly the largest flying animal ever to exist. Its wingspan was 10–11 m (11–12 yd.). When walking on the ground in search of prey, its long neck made it as tall as a giraffe.

Quetzalcoatlus lived at the end of the time of the dinosaurs. It shared the Earth with famous dinosaur giants including *Tyrannosaurus rex* and *Triceratops* (the horn-faced plant eaters that appear in our story). *Quetzalcoatlus* also lived alongside many kinds of early birds — small, feathered dinosaurs that evolved the ability to fly. *Quetzalcoatlus* probably ate animals that it could hunt on the ground, such as mammals or small dinosaurs.

Many pterosaur fossils are found near seacoasts. But fossils from *Quetzalcoatlus* and its close relatives are also found far away from the sea. They may have lived in inland habitats or migrated or flown great distances, as we show in our story.

The action in this book was inspired by an astonishing fossil discovery in Dinosaur Provincial Park in Canada. A young fossil hunter named Wendy Sloboda found a leg bone from *Quetzalcoatlus* (or possibly a close relative) that turned out to have bite marks made by a small, two-legged, meat-eating dinosaur called *Saurornitholestes* (SAW-roar-nith-o-LESS-tees). The *Saurornitholestes* even left a piece of tooth stuck in the pterosaur bone.

How did that bone wind up being chomped on by a *Saurornitholestes*? After all, *Saurornitholestes* was smaller than a wolf and much smaller than *Quetzalcoatlus*. It's possible that *Saurornitholestes* hunted large pterosaurs in packs, working together to land their prey. Or *Saurornitholestes* may simply have chewed on bones from a *Quetzalcoatlus* after it died from other causes. As with all we know about life during the time of dinosaurs, there are many questions still to be answered.